Contents

Water for life

Plants and animals need water to live.

Water makes up a large part of the bodies of all living things. Your body is about 70 per cent water, but some animals and plants contain even more.

Can you guess how much water a melon contains?

Water

Sally Morgan and Pauline Lalor

WHY WASTE IT?

SIMON & SCHUSTE
YOUNG BOOKS

This book has been prepared for
Simon & Schuster Young Books by
Globe Enterprises of Nantwich, Cheshire

Design: M&M Design Partnership
Photographs: Ecoscene except
ZEFA (15t, 15br)

First published in Great Britain in1993
by Simon & Schuster Young Books
Campus 400, Maylands Avenue
Hemel Hempstead, Herts HP2 7EZ

© 1993 Globe Enterprises

Printed and bound in Singapore
by Kim Hup Lee Printing Co Pte Ltd

A catalogue record for this book is available
from the British Library
ISBN 0 7500 1409 1

Fresh and salt water

Nearly all the water in the world is in the oceans.

The oceans contain salt water, but we can only drink fresh water. Fresh water is found in rivers, lakes and ponds.

Where does the water in rivers and lakes comes from?

Water is usually a liquid

We think of water as a liquid that we can see through and that we can pour.

When water becomes cold enough, it freezes to solid ice. If water becomes hot enough, it evaporates and disappears into the air.

How cold must it be for water to freeze? At what temperature does water boil?

Water in the home

In some parts of the world water must be collected from taps in the street or from nearby rivers or lakes.

Where does the water come from in your home? What sort of things do you use it for?

Water is fun!

Many people love playing in water or going to the beach for the day. Indoor pools are a safe place for learning to swim and for having a good time.

There are a number of other enjoyable water sports. Can you name any sports that take place under, in or on top of water?

Not enough water

In some parts of the world, it might not rain for years and there is almost no water. These places are deserts.

Plants cannot live without water. Crops must be watered if the ground is dry. Farmers take care to irrigate their fields.

Wasting water

Water is precious! There is not an endless supply even in countries where it rains often.

We must have clean water to drink, water to wash with, water for animals and crops, water for industry.

But there are ways we waste water, especially in summer. What do you think these might be?

Collecting water

Water is so valuable that we store it in reservoirs until we need it.

Sometimes we build a dam across a river to stop most of the water flowing away. A lake forms behind the dam which provides water for people living nearby. Water passing through the dam is used to make electricity.

Reservoirs have other uses.
Can you name any of them?

Dirty water

When we use water, we make it dirty.

Dirty water goes into drains and could end up in rivers and oceans. Factories may pump water into rivers and lakes without first cleaning out harmful substances.

Lakes, rivers and even seas become polluted, harming plants and animals living there.

Water can be recycled

Dirty water should be cleaned
and reused.

Even the waste water from toilets
can be cleaned at a sewage farm.
It is pumped into tanks where any
solid waste sinks to the bottom and
then slowly it drips through tanks
filled with gravel.

In the end, it is clean enough to drink.

Saving water for the future

Every year people use more and more fresh water. Soon there will not be enough for everyone.

There are ways of using less water. Showers use less than baths. Dripping taps and leaking pipes can be mended. How can water for use in the garden be collected?

Do you think there should be laws to stop people wasting water?

Saving water helps wildlife

We share our lakes and rivers with many other animals and plants.

If we waste less water there will be more left over for them. If we clean up our waste water they won't die from pollution.

Saving water, saves our planet.

Index

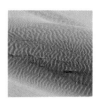